A to Z India

BY JUSTINE AND RON FONTES

children's press®

A Division of Scholastic Inc.
New York Toronto London Auckland Sydney
Mexico City New Delhi Hong Kong
Danbury, Connecticut

Series Consultant: Linda D. Bullock, Ph.D.
Series Design: Marie O'Neill
Photo Research: Candlepants Incorporated

The photos on the cover show the Taj Mahal (right), a young Indian girl in traditional dress (bottom), a lotus flower (left), and a sitar (top right).

Photographs© 2003: Corbis Images: 12 bottom, 37 top right (AFP), 9 center (Dave Bartruff), 11 (Neil Beer), 12 top (Bettmann), 31 (Gallo Images), 36 top (Lindsay Hebberd), 28 bottom (Reuters NewMedia Inc.), 6 top (Galen Rowell), cover left, 4 top (Royalty-Free), 28 top (David H. Wells), 13 right (Nevada Wier); Dinodia Picture Agency: 38 (DJD), 26 (HM), 13 left, 24 top right (HMA), 7, 30 (Sunil S. Kapadia), 6 bottom, 9 bottom, 24 bottom (Milind A. Ketkar), 17 left (H. Mahidhar), 15 (Firoze Mistay), 16 top (MMN), 8 left (R.M. Modi), 35 bottom (RS3), 14 right (Nirmala Savadekar), 22 (N.G. Sharma), 33 (SOA), 10 right (Madhusudan B. Tawde), 17 right (VHM); Hulton|Archive/Getty Images: 32; MapQuest.com, Inc.: 21; PhotoDisc/Getty Images: cover right (David Buffington), cover top (C Squared Studios); Stone/Getty Images: 9 top, 24 top left, 25 right (Anthony Cassidy), 25 left (Ben Edwards), 14 left (Paul Harris), 4 bottom (Manoj Shah); Superstock, Inc./Steve Vidler: cover bottom; Taxi/Getty Images: 29 (Peter Adams), 27 top (Gavin Hellier), 23 (Harvey Lloyd), 5 bottom (Peter Sherrard); The Image Bank/Getty Images: 19 (Macduff Everton), 34 bottom (Frans Lemmens), 10 left (Carlos Nanaias), 34 top right, 35 top left (Andrea Pistolesi), 5 top left (Art Wolfe); The Image Works: 18 (M. Amirtham/DPA), 34 top left (Dinodia), 27 bottom (DPA), 5 top right (DPA/IK), 8 right, 35 top right, 37 bottom (Hideo Haga), 36 bottom (Michael Justice), 37 top left (Christine Pemberton), 16 bottom (David Wells).
Map by XNR Productions

Library of Congress Cataloging-in-Publication Data
Fontes, Justine.
  India / by Justine and Ron Fontes.
      p. cm. – (A to Z)
Includes bibliographical references and index.
Contents: Animals – Buildings – Cities – Dress – Exports – Food –Government – History – Important people – Jobs – Keepsakes – Land – Map – Nation – Only in Mexico – People – Question – Religion – School and sports – Transportation – Unusual places – Visiting the country – Window to the past – X-tra special things – Yearly festivals – Z.
  ISBN 0-516-24564-3 (lib. bdg.)   0-516-26809-0 (pbk.)
 1. India–Juvenile literature. [1. India.] I. Fontes, Ron. II. Title. III. Series.
  DS407.F62 2003
  954'.003–dc21

                        2003006006

Contents

Elephants drinking from a waterhole

Animals

Langurs and moon moths are just a few of the strange and wonderful animals that live in India.

Langurs

Moon moths have a long tail on each wing. The moths fly toward street lights in Indian towns.

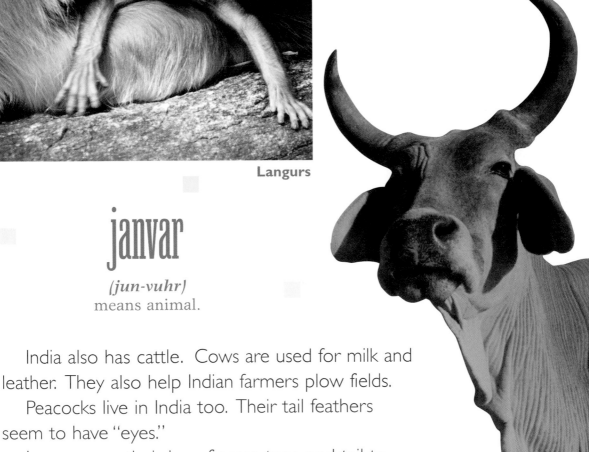

janvar

(jun-vuhr)
means animal.

India also has cattle. Cows are used for milk and leather. They also help Indian farmers plow fields.

Peacocks live in India too. Their tail feathers seem to have "eyes."

Langurs use their long fingers, toes, and tail to climb trees easily. They are also called leaf monkeys.

Taj Mahal

Buildings

The face of this building is mostly glass.

India has many modern buildings, yet its most famous building is a **tomb**.

Long ago, an Indian emperor had many wives. His favorite wife died, leaving the emperor sad. He had thousands of workers build her tomb. He wanted it to look like heaven on Earth.

It took 12 years for the workers to finish the tomb. They used marble, jewels, and more than 1,000 pounds (454 kg) of gold. It is called the **Taj Mahal**.

Mumbai has many tall, modern buildings.

Cities

Fun Fact:

More movies are made in Mumbai than in Hollywood!

In the 1500s, the Portuguese ruled a town they called Bom Bahia. That means "good bay." After the Portuguese, the British ruled the town. They called it Bombay.

Today, Bombay has a different name. It is Mumbai. Mumbai is a busy, crowded city. It is a port city that juts out into the Arabian Sea. Movies are one of its most famous businesses there. Some people call Mumbai "Bollywood." Can you guess why?

Dress

There are many different groups of people in India. Some wear clothes that are special to them.

jama

(juh-muh)
means clothing.
The English word pajamas
comes from a Hindi word
for loose pants.

Most Indian women wear a dress called a **sari**. A sari is a piece of cloth about 15 feet (5 m) long. Women wrap the cloth around their body. They wear the loose end over their shoulder or head. Saris are sometimes made from colorful silk.

Men wear long cloths, too. They tie the cloth around their head to make a **turban**. They also wear loose white pants called **dhoti**. They wrap a long cloth around their hips and between their legs.

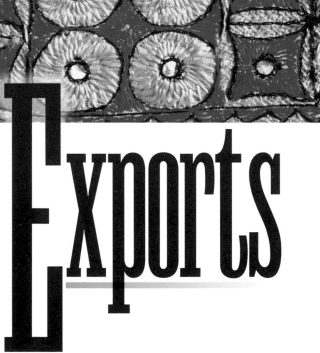

Exports

Tea leaves are bright green on the bush. They are picked and dried. Sometimes, spices are added.

Indian farmers grow lots of tea, which is **exported**. More than one million people work on large tea farms. In the wild, tea bushes can grow 10 feet (3 m) tall. Farmers must cut the bushes often to make it easier to pick leaves.

Beautiful cloth, beads, jewelry, and computer software are also important exports.

Curry Butter

WHAT YOU NEED:
- 1 stick unsalted butter, at room temperature
- 1 1/2 teaspoons curry powder
- 1 tablespoon lime or lemon juice
- 1/2 teaspoon ground ginger

HOW TO MAKE IT:
Mix everything together in a bowl. Empty the bowl onto a piece of plastic wrap. Use the wrap to mold the butter into a log. Let it get cold in the refrigerator.

Food

Indians cook with lots of spices, including **curry**. For a taste of India, add curry butter to your favorite dish. Ask an adult to help you make some curry butter using this recipe.

Indira Gandhi was India's first female prime minister. Her father, Jawaharlal Nehru, was India's first prime minister.

Government

Here, Prime Minister Atal Behari Vajpayee (left) meets with President A.P.J. Abdul Kalam.

In India, people vote for their leaders. They choose a president. The president chooses a prime minister. The prime minister is the head of the government.

The **Parliament** makes laws for India. Laws are sent to the president to sign.

Parliament has two "houses," or parts. Voters choose most of the people in one house.

India has 28 states and 7 territories. The states have governments, too. India's president chooses the governor for each state. These governments choose people to serve in the second house of Parliament.

In the past, emperors wore the finest jewels. Jewels were made with gold, pearls, rubies, diamonds, and other valuable stones.

History

Siddhartha founded the religion Buddhism. Later, he became known as Buddha. There are many statues of Buddha in India.

India's first emperor had a son named Ashoka. Ashoka fought battles to make his father's empire bigger. In time, Ashoka stopped fighting. He became a **Buddhist**.

Ashoka wrote his beliefs on rocks and statues for others to read. He told people to respect other people's religions. He also told them to give to the poor and not kill animals.

M. F. Husain painted a portrait of Satyajit Ray, who is an Indian film director.

Many artists live in Calcutta.

Important People

Ravi Shankar helped spread Indian music to countries around the world.

Much of India's early music was not written. Musicians taught their students how to play. Then the students taught students of their own. Today, there are many schools of music. Ravi Shankar brought ancient Indian music to places like the United States. He plays the **sitar**, a musical instrument with strings that came from India.

M. F. Husain is one of India's famous artists. As a young man, Husain painted large movie posters on walls. He soon became famous around the world.

kalakar

(kuh-luh-huhr)
means artist.

Jobs

Many people who live on the coasts make their living as fishers.

Today, more and more Indians are working in technology. Bangalore is a growing city and technology center.

Most Indians are farmers. People in the cities work in offices and factories. Metals like iron and steel come from steel mills. In factories, people turn the metals into machines, including airplanes, cars, and bicycles.

Other people work in cotton mills. Cotton is turned into clothing that people around the world wear.

Computer jobs are becoming very important in India too. People in the cities use computers in their work. They visit computer cafes in their free time.

People enjoy watching and participating in kite fights.

Keepsakes

Flying kites is popular in India. On January 14, there are kite festivals. The festival celebrates the end of winter. Expert kite flyers come from around the world.

In ancient India, people who pretended to be someone else could be put to death. So people didn't act to tell stories, they used puppets instead. These puppets showed Indian gods, horses, elephants, cows, birds, and deer.

Hogenakal Fall

Land

pahar
(puh-huhr)
means mountain.

India has all kinds of land. There are mountains capped with snow. There are valleys and forests. There are flat plains and deserts, too.

Rubber is made from the sap of rubber trees. The trees grow on big farms, or plantations.

The Indian Ocean touches India on the east, west, and south. The Himalayas are in the north and are the tallest mountains in the world. The word *Himalaya* means "house of snow" in **Sanskrit**, the ancient language of India.

The Thar Desert is in the west. People who live here need camels to get around. In the east, India gets heavy rains called **monsoons**.

There are nine rivers that are holy to Indian people. The Ganges and Kaveri Rivers are two of them.

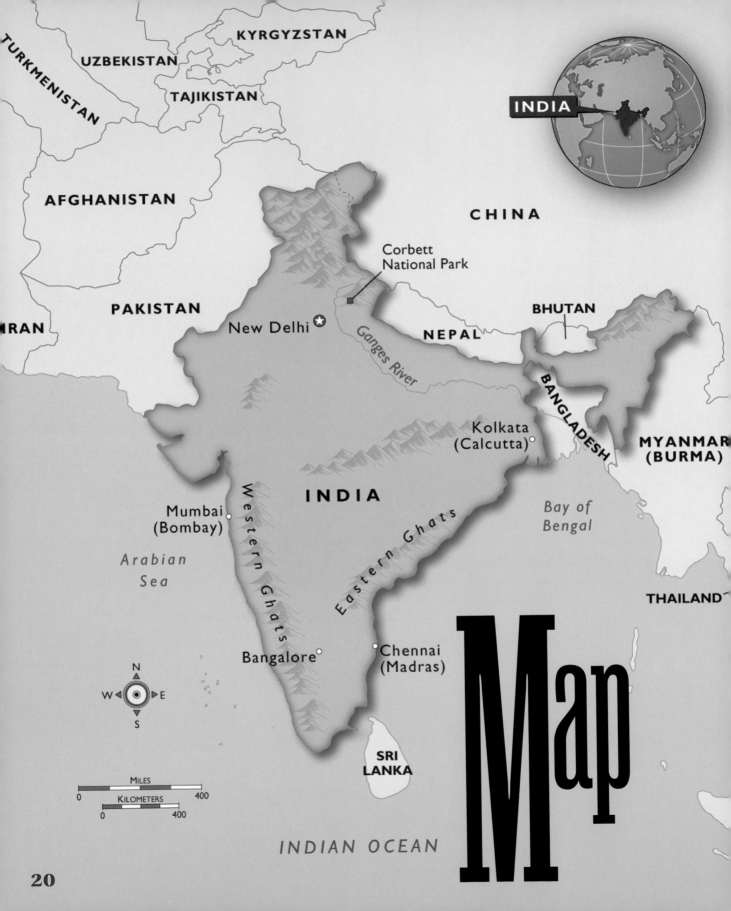

KYRGYZSTAN

TURKMENISTAN

UZBEKISTAN

TAJIKISTAN

INDIA

AFGHANISTAN

CHINA

IRAN

PAKISTAN

Corbett
National Park

New Delhi ✪

NEPAL

BHUTAN

Ganges River

BANGLADESH

MYANMAR
(BURMA)

Kolkata
(Calcutta)

INDIA

Bay of
Bengal

Mumbai
(Bombay)

Arabian
Sea

Western Ghats

Eastern Ghats

THAILAND

Bangalore

Chennai
(Madras)

Map

N
W ◄◉► E
S

SRI
LANKA

MILES
0   400
KILOMETERS
0   400

INDIAN OCEAN

Nation

India's flag has three stripes. The top stripe is dark orange. Beneath it are two stripes of white and green.

The dark orange stands for courage. The white stands for peace. The green stands for faith.

There is a blue wheel in the center of the white stripe. This wheel is a Buddhist symbol called the **Dharma Chakra**. The wheel has 24 spokes. These spokes stand for the hours in a day. The wheel helps people remember that life is always moving forward.

Visitors to Little Rann of Kutch can take a camel safari, or journey.

Only in India

Special places, stories, music, and dance help keep India's long history alive.

Kathakali means "story play." For 400 years, dancers in Kerala have told stories of good and evil without speaking. Male dancers wear wide, colorful skirts, fancy headdresses, and jewelry. It takes hours for dancers to put on their makeup.

The Little Rann of Kutch is a special place you'll find only in India. Swamps and grassy islands form here from the monsoon rains. Unusual animals live here, like wolves and cats called **caracals**.

23

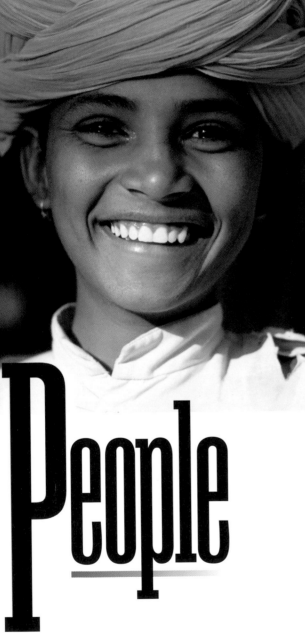

Most Indians still live in small villages in the countryside.

People

India is the seventh largest country in the world. More than one billion people live there.

Large families often live together in one home. Families include grandparents, parents, aunts, uncles, and children. Many parents choose husbands and wives for their children. Married women usually live with their husband's family.

The people in India speak hundreds of different languages. Most speak **Hindi**. English also helps some people from different parts of India speak to each other. Movies are made in 15 different languages. Schools teach almost 60 languages. Newspapers are written in almost 90 languages.

Question

What are snake charmers?

People once believed that snake charmers could tame dangerous snakes like cobras. Snake charmers carried covered baskets from village to village. They stopped to play their flutes. As they played, a snake rose from the basket. The snake swayed back and forth. It seemed to move with the flute's music, as if under a spell.

People now know snakes can't hear the flute's music, they only follow its movement.

Hindus believe the Ganges River is holy.
They bathe in it to wash away sins.

Religion

Mahatma Gandhi helped India
become free from the rule of
Great Britain.

Most Indians are Hindus. Hinduism began in India about 4,000 years ago. The religion has no single god or special book. It has many gods and beliefs. Hindu people search for ways to live a good life. This search is called *dharma*.

Hindus worship in different ways. Some pray or sit quietly. They also celebrate their religion with festivals. They believe in peace and understanding for all people.

27

School & Sports

Schools are free and open to all children. In most Indian states, children must go to school. Yet many children do not go because they must help their families. Half of Indians cannot read, but that is changing.

Cricket is an important sport in India. So is soccer. Many Indians enjoy flying kites and playing board games. The games of chess and Parcheesi come from India.

A cricket game needs two teams of 11 players and a special bat.

28

Taxi *phat-phats* are usually all yellow, all black, or both colors.

Transportation

There are many ways to get around India. Some people travel by car. Others fly in planes. Still others use trains. India has more miles of railroad tracks than most countries in the world.

In cities and villages, people ride bicycles and motorcycles. Many also take a ride in a crowded bus or in a rickshaw. A rickshaw is a cart that is pulled by a person or an animal. Some rickshaws have motors. These speedy rickshaws are called *phat-phats*.

29

Unusual Places

Indian artists made the 34 amazing caves at Ellora. They are filled with paintings and statues of gods and goddesses that tell stories from three religions.

One of the most amazing caves is the Kailasanatha Temple. Carved in a cliff, this huge temple shows a mountain where the Hindu god, Lord Shiva, lived. Artists built a tall tower to stand for the mountain. Two life-sized elephant statues also stand in the courtyard.

More than 100 tigers live in the park.
The park was India's first safe place for tigers.

Visiting the Country

Corbett National Park is India's first national park. Under British rule, the park was for hunters. Today, it is a safe place for animals to live.

You can go to the tops of watchtowers around the park and see many kinds of birds. You can see antelopes. You can watch gharials, a kind of crocodile, walk along muddy riverbanks. At sunrise and sunset, you can take a ride on an elephant to see leopards and tigers.

These women play a sport called *kalari payat*. It is an ancient Indian martial art, or kind of fighting.

Window to the Past

Traditions stay alive in small towns and villages. Some people dress differently. Others work or play in old ways.

Young Buddhist monks

Monks are religious people who leave their homes and families to live, work, and pray together.

Monks have lived in India for many hundreds of years. Long ago, they learned special ways to fight to protect themselves from thieves. These ways of fighting are called **martial arts**. Now, people around the world practice martial arts.

Today, people can visit many of the places where monks live. They can watch monks worship like they did in ancient times.

X-tra Special Things

This man has one of the world's longest moustaches.

People use giant dolls to act out the story of Rama. Indians believe Rama was their god Vishnu come to Earth again.

Jodhpur is called "the blue city." That's because many of its houses are painted blue. The light blue color reflects sunlight. That helps people stay cool, even in the hot winds that blow from the Thar Desert nearby.

There is a **bazaar** in the old part of "The Blue City." Shopkeepers sell jangling bracelets, colorful cotton cloth, and puppets. You can smell candy and spices in the air. Artists in the bazaar use **henna**, a dye, to decorate the hands of Indian women.

These cows roam Varanasi, India's holiest city. Indians say they are holy and do not eat their meat.

35

Diwali

Yearly Festivals

Indians celebrate many religious holidays. They also hold festivals to celebrate crops, animals, and the seasons.

All over India, people hold a Holi festival, or Festival of Color. It celebrates the end of winter. The holiday starts with bonfires at night. The next day, people wear white clothes. They crowd the streets to spray colored water and powder on each other. There is singing and dancing everywhere.

The birthday of the god Krishna is also celebrated. Pots of butter hang from strings in the sky. People stand in human pyramids to try to reach the pots.

People spend hours decorating elephants to march in the Elephant Festival.

Zeera

Today, cooks around the world use *zeera*, or cumin, in their dishes.

masala

(muh-suh-luh)
means spice.

Zeera is a spice that grows in India. In English, the spice is called cumin. The plant's tiny seeds are ground into powder. The powder is added to all kinds of foods to make them tastier.

Zeera isn't the only spice in Indian food. Indians have grown and sold spices since ancient times. Traders came by land and sea to buy spices like cinnamon, cloves, nutmeg, pepper, ginger, and saffron.

Spices are also mixed together. Curry is made from cumin, mustard, peppers, and other spices.

Hindi and English Words

bazaar (buh-ZAR) an outdoor market

Buddhist (BOO-dist) a follower of Buddhism, an Asian religion that teaches rising above earthly desires

caracal (KAR-uh-kuhl) a lynx-like cat with long, black ear tufts that lives in parts of Africa, Asia, and India

chakra (chu-kruh) the Sanskrit word for wheel

curry (KUH-ree) a mix of cumin, turmeric, and other spice powders used to flavor hot dishes called curries usually served over rice

dharma (dhuhr-muh) right behavior, Hindu law, the Buddhist truth

dhoti (dhoh-tye) the loincloth worn by male Hindus

export (EK-sport) to send products to another country for sale

henna (HEN-uh) a dye for hair and skin made from a tropical shrub

Hindi (HIN-dee) one of the offical languages of India

jama (juh-muh) Hindi word for clothing

janvar (juhn-vuhr) Hindi word for animal

kalakar (kuh-luh-kuhr) Hindi word for artist

martial art (MAR-shuhl ART) a method of self-defense, a fighting sport like karate or judo

monsoon (mon-SOON) a very strong wind that blows across the Indian Ocean and southern Asia, bringing heavy rains in summer and hot, dry weather in winter

pahar (puh-huhr) Hindi word for mountain

parliament (PAR-luh-muhnt) the group of people elected to make laws in certain countries

safari (suh-FAH-ree) a journey, often taken to photograph or hunt large, wild animals

Sanskrit the ancient, sacred language of the Hindus in India

sari (SAH-ree) the dress worn by many Indian women made from a long piece of light fabric wrapped around the body and over one shoulder

sitar (SIH-tare) an Indian stringed instrument with a very long neck

Taj Mahal a beautiful and famous tomb in northern India finished in 1643

tomb (toom) a house or chamber built for someone who has died

technology (tek-NOL-uh-jee) the use of science and engineering to solve practical problems

turban (TUR-buhn) the headdress often worn by Indian and Arab men made by winding a long scarf around the head or a cap

Let's Explore More

A Child's Day in an Indian Village (Child's Day) by Prodeepta Das, Benchmark Books, 2001

Look What Came From India by Miles Harvey, Franklin Watts, 1999

India (Picture a Country) by Henry Pluckrose, Franklin Watts, 1999

Websites

www.atozkidsstuff.com/india.html
Learn about India's animals, flag, history, play games, and read folktales.

www.indias.com
Get the latest news from India, plus information and links on topics like fashion, sports, science, and more.

www.kidsfortigers.org
Learn what kids in India and on the web are doing to help save tigers.

Index

Italic page numbers indicate illustrations.

Meet the Authors

JUSTINE & RON FONTES have written nearly 400 children's books together. Since 1988, they have published *critter news*, a free newsletter that keeps them in touch with publishers from their home in Maine.

The Fonteses have written many biographies and early readers, as well as historical novels and other books combining facts with stories. Their love of animals is expressed in the nature notes columns of *critter news*.

During his childhood in Tennessee, Ron was a member of the Junior Classical League and went on to tutor Latin students. At 16, Ron was drawing a science fiction comic strip for the local newspaper. A professional artist for 30 years, Ron has also been in theater as a costumer, makeup artist, and designer.

Justine was born in New York City and worked in publishing while earning a BA in English Literature Phi Beta Kappa from New York University. Thanks to her parents' love of travel, Justine visited most of Europe as a child, going as far north as Finland. During college, she spent time in France and Spain.